"*Struggles don't come with a notice, and no one would choose them if they did. Vet, it's in these unannounced battles that we uncover our greatest strength and resilience.*"

THE POWER OF TRANSITION:

"DESTINY TRANSITION VS. STAGED TRANSITION"

(Understanding and Overcoming Destiny Struggles)

S. OLAMILEKAN ISREAL

THE POWER OF TRANSITION

Copyright © 2024 By S. Olamilekan Isreal

All rights reserved.

S. Olamilekan Isreal
The President, The Light of Israel services
Website: www.olamilekanisreal.com

Editor: Mr. Kolade Gbolagade

ISBN: 978-978-772-962-5(Paperback)
       978-978-772-963-2(eBook)

Table of Contents

PREFACE:

The Power of Transition:
"Destiny Transition vs. Staged Transition"

Life is a journey marked by inevitable transitions. Some we anticipate, and others catch us off guard. These moments, while often challenging, define the trajectory of our lives. My personal story is one of navigating these phases, facing struggles that sometimes felt insurmountable. I have had moments when the weight of my challenges threatened to crush me. And yet, I have emerged more robust, not by my power alone but through divine intervention and the grace that carried me when I could not bring myself to.

During these experiences, I noticed a profound truth: transitions, though painful, hold the key to transformation. I also observed others walking similar paths. Some triumphed, while others faltered not for lack of effort but because life's challenges overwhelmed them. These stories, both of victory and heartbreak, inspired me to write this book.

Why Does This Book Matter?

The transitions we experience can be divided into "Staged Transitions" and "Destiny Transitions."

Staged Transitions: These are struggles imposed by external factors, not meant to shape us but to derail our purpose. They may arise from economic conditions, societal values, family influences, or spiritual forces. These staged struggles have often been overlooked yet have derailed countless destinies.

Destiny Transitions: These are challenges and growth periods that align with our true purpose and are designed to strengthen and prepare us for our ordained path.

Understanding the difference between these two types of transitions is essential for navigating life's challenges. This book will guide you through both.

A Journey Through Struggle and Triumph

For years, I wondered why some people seemed to overcome monumental obstacles while others, equally talented and driven, fell short. Why do some rise from their struggles to build legacies while others leave unrealised potential? This book seeks to answer that question. It does not just celebrate those who succeeded. It honours those who tried valiantly but did not make it.

Their stories are often overlooked, but they hold potent lessons. We need to learn from their struggles, perseverance, and humanity. These individuals fought hard against their transitions, and while they may not have reached their goals, their courage deserves to be remembered.

This book also celebrates triumphs—those who embraced their destiny transitions and emerged stronger, wiser, and more impactful. Figures like Nelson Mandela, Martin Luther King Jr., and Bishop David Oyedepo did not bypass their struggles; they walked through them gracefully and purposefully. Their stories inspire us to press on, even when the path is steep.

A Roadmap for Your Journey

"The Power of Transition" is not just a collection of stories but also a guide. Within these pages, you will find practical strategies to help you:

- **Recognise** whether you are in a staged transition or a destiny transition.
- **Understand** the purpose of each phase and how it contributes to your growth.
- **Overcome** the challenges that threaten to derail your journey.

This book equips you with the tools to face your transitions head-on. You will learn how to harness your struggles, build resilience, and lean on the support systems around you. You will also discover how to embrace your divine destiny and use your journey to inspire and uplift others.

A Call to Action

Transitions are not the end; they are the beginning of something greater. If you are in the middle of a struggle, know this: you are not alone. Your pain has a purpose, and your perseverance will pay off.

This book is for those who feel stuck during their transitions, those who have given up hope, and those who are holding on by a thread. It is for anyone who wants to turn their pain into purpose and their struggles into strength.

Let us honour those who came before us, those who triumphed, and those who fell along the way. Let us learn from their journeys and be inspired by their courage. And let us embrace our transitions, knowing that they shape us into the people we were always meant to be.

As you read these pages, may you find hope, strength, and the tools to navigate your transitions gracefully and purposefully. Your journey matters, and your legacy is waiting to be built. Amen!

✳ 1 ✳

Understanding Life's Crossroads:
Destiny Transitions vs. Staged Transitions

As a child, I often questioned what was happening in my country. I would ask my parents deep questions, only to be met with silence, criticism, or dismissal. It was not their fault entirely—they held tightly to their beliefs and avoided questioning, fearing it might seem culturally or spiritually disrespectful. So, I learned through my mistakes, understanding the weight of consequences.

Growing up, I faced situations that felt like training grounds for my potential, preparing me for a greater purpose. However, many of my struggles were not due to poor planning or lack of discipline. Instead, they stemmed from factors beyond my control, such as economic conditions, cultural values, family background, spiritual forces, and limited financial support. While many great leaders have overcome hardships to reach their destinies, I could not ignore those who, despite being destined for greatness, never reached it. Their unfulfilled potential deserves attention.

We must examine what holds back these destined leaders, why they remain forgotten, and what caused them to veer from their paths. Some were ridiculed or shamed, others rejected, and all were left to bear the burden of unrealised dreams. After my own experiences, I started searching for answers. One key factor and ignored force I found was "Staged Transition."

What is "Staged Transitions?"

Staged Transitions are struggles imposed by external factors, not meant to shape us but to derail our purpose. These may arise from economic conditions, societal values, family influences, or spiritual forces. These staged struggles have often been overlooked yet derailed countless destinies.

I often say that if Joseph, the biblical figure who became chancellor of Egypt by 30, had grown up where I did, in my family and environment, he may not have reached that position so quickly, if at all. This is not to question his destiny but to illustrate how deeply our society can impact us. Many spiritual battles are beyond even the strongest anointing or innate potential. Joseph's success, I believe, was possible because he encountered "Destiny Transitions" rather than "Staged Transitions."

What is "Destiny Transitions?"

Destiny Transitions are challenging, and growth phases are embedded in our lives to prepare us for our ultimate purpose. These are the struggles that, from birth, God has woven into our journey to refine us and enable us to achieve our true destiny.

I grew up in a culture where misfortunes are met with silence, in a society that sometimes tolerates corruption, and where fear of evil prevents us from challenging wrongdoing. In a nation where systems and policies seem rigged to benefit the unscrupulous, achieving one's destiny can feel like an uphill battle.

So, how do we pursue our destiny in such a society? We need to start by asking hard questions and acknowledging these obstacles. There are societies where the challenges are even more significant but rarely come to light. Confronting and understanding these forces is the first step to rising above them and moving closer to our purpose.

I once came across a blog by Jack Canfield titled "The Formula That Puts You in Control of Success." In it, he emphasises a powerful truth: we are each "100% responsible for our lives—the good and the bad." He highlights the importance of self-discipline in shaping our future. While I resonate with Canfield's message, his advice especially applies to a society like the United States. In many other parts of the world, particularly in underdeveloped nations, success often involves external factors beyond individual control.

For example, I had a high school classmate named Michael Obong. He struggled academically, so our teachers questioned whether he even belonged in school. He was eventually advised to withdraw despite his parents' desperate pleas. Years later, I reconnected with Michael on LinkedIn and was astonished to see that he had not only turned his life around but also earned impressive professional qualifications. I could not help but ask him what had made the difference.

Michael shared that after moving to the U.S., he noticed a remarkable improvement in his memory and understanding of things that had seemed impossible back home in Nigeria. He attributed this change to two primary factors: a different cultural and systemic environment and freedom from the "family spiritual forces" that had held his family back from academic success. While he had prayed and fasted countless times in Nigeria, his struggles persisted until he left the country.

This story highlights an important truth: success principles can vary greatly depending on the context. Spiritual beliefs, societal systems, and family dynamics can significantly impact an individual's progress. What may work in one place may face insurmountable obstacles in another. It is a reminder that achieving success is not always as straightforward as it seems.

Research also reveals how external factors shape the ability to reach one's full potential. Studies show that economic status alone accounts for about 25% of the differences in educational and career outcomes, as limited finances restrict access to quality resources (Harvard Gazette). Poor social policies reduce opportunities by 20-30%, especially in regions with weak educational and social systems, limiting upward mobility (Fordham Institute).

Structural issues in healthcare and education—especially in areas with poor infrastructure—can decrease achievement potential by 15-20%. Cultural and spiritual beliefs also shape values and expectations, often influencing achievement by ten to 15%, depending on societal norms. Family background, particularly socio-economic status, remains one of the most significant predictors of success, accounting for 30-40% of the barriers faced by children from lower-income families (Harvard Gazette and Fordham Institute). These factors clearly show how deeply external influences shape our journey.

Despite these challenges, many still look to religious texts like the Bible for inspiration and hope. However, I believe that actual productivity goes beyond the literal interpretation of these texts. Those who are both religious and truly productive focus not just on faith but on applying sound principles that drive tangible outcomes.

I recall a passage in 2 Kings where the prophet Elisha proclaimed in Samaria, *"By this time tomorrow, a measure of fine flour will be sold for a shekel."* This prophecy came to pass through the actions of four lepers. There was even a man who doubted the prophecy and suffered the consequences.

While this story shows the power of faith, I have not seen an economy turn around simply because someone spoke a prophecy. Fundamental economic transformation requires more than just proclamations. It demands the application of principles, policies, and systemic changes. Though I have personally experienced miracles, I firmly believe that lasting economic progress results from consistent, dedicated effort and not simply waiting for a miraculous intervention.

Recognising the Forces of Destiny and Staged Transition

Understanding the distinction between "Destiny Transition" and "Staged Transition" is crucial to navigating life's challenges. Many people view their struggles as unchangeable destinies, overlooking the practical strategies that could propel them forward. By recognising the forces at play, we can understand when to embrace our circumstances, adapt to change, or take proactive steps to implement solutions, ultimately conserving our time, energy, and resources while increasing productivity.

As we close this chapter, let us reflect on the profound power of understanding these transition forces in our lives. Every challenge, whether it feels inevitable or within our control, holds the potential to shape us in unique and powerful ways. By knowing when to embrace, adapt, or strategise, we empower ourselves to move forward with greater clarity and purpose.

Believe that you can overcome obstacles, grow, and transform. Trust your journey, knowing that destiny and staged transition are not just forces shaping you but opportunities to fuel your growth. As you step into the next chapter, carry this wisdom with you, ready to face each transition with resilience and the confidence that your best self is waiting ahead.

In the next chapter, we will delve into "Destiny Transition" and how it prepares us for success and helps us unlock our true potential.

* 2 *

Destiny Transitions:
The Path to Purpose

The story of Joseph in the Bible provides a powerful example of "Destiny transition," a journey where struggles and challenges play a critical role in leading to success. Joseph faced betrayal by his brothers, enslavement, and prison, yet these hardships shaped his character. When he finally rose to power as Egypt's prime minister, he used his wisdom to save the nation from famine. Joseph's story illustrates that destiny transitions often include obstacles that, rather than hindering us, equip us for a higher purpose.

This theme appears in the lives of many modern figures who faced adversity and emerged stronger. Mahatma Gandhi encountered imprisonment and immense opposition while fighting for India's independence. Despite this, he remained steadfast, transforming his struggles into the strength that led to India's liberation and inspired global movements for justice. Similarly, Nelson Mandela's 27 years in prison only deepened his resolve; he emerged to lead South Africa's unification under democracy, ending apartheid with a vision forged through hardship.

Elon Musk's ventures into electric vehicles and space exploration faced scepticism and financial hurdles. Yet his persistence through failure exemplifies how destiny transitions may seem impossible but are often essential for groundbreaking success. Jeff Bezos also faced doubts when he started Amazon, yet through adaptation and resilience, he built one of the world's largest e-commerce empires.

Donald Trump's journey also illustrates resilience, as he overcame numerous business and personal challenges before eventually pivoting to politics and becoming the 45th and 47th President of the United States. Dr. Ben Carson's path, marked by limited resources and educational obstacles, led him to become a renowned neurosurgeon, pioneering surgeries that changed medical history.

The story of Job in the Bible is another example of a profound destiny transition. Job endured tremendous loss, from his wealth to his health, yet he maintained faith and resilience. His story concludes with God restoring him, giving him twice as much as he had before. Job's life teaches us that after struggles or adversity often come growth opportunities.

These individuals, like Joseph and Job, experienced their own form of destiny transition, where obstacles became catalysts for growth. These journeys remind us that destiny transitions do not bring us to defeat; they position us for resilience, purpose, and eventual success. By embracing these transitions as opportunities for growth, we can transform hardship into stepping stones, aligning with a path that fulfils our higher purpose.

Signs That Show You're on a Path That Aligns with Your Purpose

One clear sign that shows you're on the right path is when challenges and setbacks fuel growth and open doors to new opportunities. A purpose-driven path transforms struggles into stepping stones, equipping you with the tools and resilience to thrive. If you consistently see personal development, enhanced skills, or increased confidence from your trials, these transitions will likely shape you for tremendous success.

However, it may be time to re-evaluate your path if you are stuck in repeated, stagnant cycles without progress. Growth and purpose are closely tied; a path aligned with your purpose should inspire you to evolve despite hardship. Other signs include:

1. **Inner Peace and Fulfilment:** Even in tough times, you feel a sense of peace or fulfilment.
2. **Resilience and Resourcefulness:** You bounce back with renewed focus and solutions despite setbacks.
3. **Connection and Alignment:** People, opportunities, and experiences align with your values and goals.
4. **Progress Over Perfection:** You see consistent growth, learning from each experience.

When these signs are present, they indicate you're on a purposeful path. Trusting these signals can help you stay committed, knowing each step forward shapes you into who you're meant to become.

How Destiny Transitions Enhance Potential and Prepare You for Success

Destiny transitions are the pivotal challenges and redirections we encounter, shaping us into who we are meant to become. Many people use age or wealth to measure success, but these can be misleading. Actual growth comes from lessons within life experiences and how we adapt to them.

Destiny transitions carry us through hardships that refine our character, build resilience, and deepen our understanding. Personally, my journey was filled with obstacles, including repeated setbacks in my education. After high school, I enrolled in multiple universities but had to drop out due to financial struggles. When I finally had a chance to study abroad, I fell seriously ill during my first semester, forcing me to return home. Back home, I faced more problems and was held back for months. Years later, after overcoming these barriers, I completed my MBA and earned Leadership and Theology Degrees, and today, I am pursuing a Ph.D. My path, filled with frustration, ultimately led to fulfilment, a testament to the transformative power of destiny transitions. Each hardship taught me resilience, resourcefulness, and patience, which are essential to my growth and success.

Recognising Signs of a Destiny Transition

If you find yourself in challenging circumstances that, despite the difficulty, seem to sharpen your skills and prepare you for more significant goals, you might be in a destiny transition. Signs include:

1. **Growth through Challenges:** Struggles are met with personal growth or new skills.

2. **Inner Resolve:** Your sense of purpose strengthens as external circumstances push against you.

3. **Unusual Persistence of Challenges:** Repeated obstacles may indicate a refining process rather than mere bad luck.

Destiny transitions reveal resilience, clarify purpose, and enhance potential. Learning to embrace them can be one of life's most valuable lessons. From my own story, had I given up on my education, I wouldn't be here, sharing insights that might change lives. As we navigate these transitions, we develop the strength and skills we need to fulfil our future purpose. Each experience prepares us for new opportunities, ultimately leading to a life of purpose and impact.

Life's most profound growth often emerges from its most significant challenges. Destiny transitions test us, but they also transform us, turning each hardship into a stepping stone towards a higher purpose. Embrace these moments, knowing they are not pushing you to give up but guiding you to become the person you're meant to be. Trust the process, and let each transition bring you closer to your destiny.

* 3 *

The Challenges Within
Destiny Transitions

It was one of those peaceful Saturday evenings when the world felt just a little quieter. My wife and I lounged on the couch, scrolling through Netflix for something to watch. We had just finished a series we had been following for weeks, and now we were hunting for something equally captivating. That was when we stumbled upon "Maid," a series that caught our attention with its raw premise and intriguing cast, including Margaret Qualley and Nick Robinson as Alex and Sean.

The story pulled us in immediately. It wasn't just entertainment; it was an emotional journey. Alex, a young mother, escapes an abusive relationship with her daughter, Maddy, in tow. What follows is a relentless fight against homelessness, legal battles, and the crushing weight of societal judgment. Her life seems to be an endless series of uphill climbs, but her determination to create a better life for her daughter shines through in every scene. It wasn't just about survival; it was about transformation.

What hit me hardest was the authenticity of Alex's struggles. She wasn't painted as a superhero but as a deeply flawed, profoundly human individual navigating impossible odds. Her courage and resilience became her superpowers, enabling her to move forward even when the system seemed determined to hold her back. Along the way, she found unexpected friendships and rediscovered her passion for writing—a lifeline that helped her reclaim her voice and future.

After the credits rolled, I turned to my wife with a question gnawing at me: "What if Alex's story had played out in our society? Do you think she would have come through it as quickly?" My wife gave me a knowing smile and laughed. "Not likely," she said, and her reasoning struck a chord. "Here, she'd face more than just broken systems. She'd deal with unstable leadership, deep economic struggles, and even spiritual battles."

Her answer hit me like a revelation. Indeed, our society often adds layers of complexity that make escaping adversity even harder. In Alex's world, her journey was a "Destiny Transition," where she drew on her inner strength to fight through external barriers. But in many places, transitions are more about surviving the stages imposed by society: oppressive systems, weak governance, and cultural stigmas that can derail progress.

The difference between these two kinds of transitions was glaring. Alex's story wasn't just about getting by; it was about becoming. She evolved from a victim of her circumstances into the architect of her own destiny. Her journey was a powerful reminder that while systems and circumstances shape us, our inner resilience is the ultimate game-changer.

As I reflected on her story that night, I realised it wasn't just fiction. It was a mirror—a reflection of the struggles so many people face and the strength they need to rise above them. Alex's journey serves as proof of one thing: no matter how hard life gets, there is always a way forward if we are willing to fight for it.

The journey of pursuing a meaningful path often tests us in profound ways. I remember my struggles while writing my first book, "It's Not God, It's You!" Doubts and setbacks were constant companions, and there were days I felt utterly alone. Financial pressures weighed heavily on me, and my dedication to this calling clashed with the pressing need to support my family. Society didn't understand my vision; some even mocked it. Without a publisher, I had to rely solely on myself, my family, and a few close friends who believed in my mission.

Despite the doubts and difficulties, I kept going. Each obstacle became a stepping stone, and the unwavering support of my fantastic wife helped me push forward. After the struggle of self-publishing, I faced even more challenges. Friends and acquaintances I expected would celebrate my work barely acknowledged it, yet unexpectedly, strangers reached out with words of encouragement, showing me that resilience and faith truly can move mountains.

I have self-published my second book and am already deep into my third, "The Power of a Collective Mindset." I'm driven by a lifelong desire to make a difference, to uplift and impact people wherever I go. The joy of inspiring others is what keeps me going and fuels every word I write. If not for this purpose, I may have given up long ago. But I know that with every challenge overcome, I am one step closer to creating a lasting impact.

Let this chapter be a testament: even when the path is lonely, the vision blurry, and the challenges daunting, if you hold onto a purpose that moves you, there's nothing you cannot overcome. Embrace each struggle; let it refine you, and keep pressing forward. Your light will find its way to those who need it most.

Understanding Destiny Transitions

Destiny transitions are profound, life-altering shifts that pull us towards our true purpose. They often arrive without warning and challenge us to redefine ourselves. Unlike anticipated changes, destiny transitions feel inevitable, calling us forward into new phases of growth and self-discovery. They bring unique challenges that can test our resilience, spark self-doubt, and require courage.

1. **Facing Self-Doubt and Emotional Turmoil:** One of the first hurdles in a destiny transition is confronting self-doubt. Shifting into a new role or following a calling often stirs questions like, "Am I enough for this?" or "Can I do this?" If left unchecked, self-doubt can become paralysing, creating cycles of insecurity. Beyond doubt, destiny transitions may bring emotional upheaval. Stepping towards a new purpose often means leaving behind familiarity with jobs, routines, or relationships. This disruption can trigger sadness, fear, or regret as we confront the parts of ourselves that we must leave behind.

    - **Overcoming Self-Doubt:** Acknowledge doubt as part of the journey. Practices like journalling, seeking mentors, or simply sharing your fears with trusted confidants can help validate and clarify your feelings. Remember, destiny doesn't demand perfection; it merely requires faith and a willingness to grow.

2. **Letting Go of the Past:** We often must shed habits, environments, or relationships that no longer align with our direction to step into a new calling. This process can feel like a personal loss. Moving on from a stable job, re-evaluating relationships, or changing daily routines can feel like losing parts of ourselves.

    Letting go often brings grief, but it is a necessary step in making room for new growth and opportunities. We grieve the familiar comforts of the past, but this process allows us to embrace the unknown with open arms.

    - **Moving Beyond the Past:** Focus on gratitude for the experiences that shaped you and visualise the possibilities ahead. Creating a small ritual, such as writing a farewell letter to your old self, can bring closure and mark a significant step in your journey.

3. **Isolation and Misunderstanding:** Destiny transitions can sometimes feel isolating, especially when those close to us don't understand our new path. Family, friends, or colleagues may question our choices, leaving us feeling unsupported or judged. Yet, pursuing a purpose requires moments of solitude, allowing us to strengthen our convictions and find new communities aligned with our vision.

    - **Creating a Support System:** Seek out like-minded individuals who share your journey. Join communities or engage with groups where your passion is understood, whether online, in person, or through inspiring books and stories. Finding such support can provide reassurance and a sense of belonging.

4. **Overcoming Unexpected Obstacles with Resilience:** Destiny transitions often bring unexpected challenges, like financial hardships or logistical barriers, that can feel like tests. These obstacles seem like detours, but they are opportunities to build resilience and deepen commitment. Each setback can add to our story, reminding us of our strength and dedication.

5. **Maintaining Faith and Trust in the Journey:** Above all, navigating a destiny transition requires unwavering faith. Faith in a higher purpose, ourselves, or the journey itself. Trusting that each step, even the setbacks, brings us closer to our calling is essential.

   - **Cultivating Faith:** Engage in practices that nurture trust, whether meditation, prayer, affirmations, or journalling. Reflecting on small victories or lessons learned reminds us how far we have come and strengthens our faith in the journey ahead.

Real-Life Stories of Destiny Transitions

1. Oprah Winfrey: Transforming Adversity into Purpose

Oprah Winfrey's life is a powerful example of destiny emerging from adversity. Born into poverty, she faced abuse and early struggles with self-worth. Despite these challenges, she pursued a career in broadcasting, enduring setbacks and rejections. Through determination, she eventually became a celebrated talk show host, inspiring millions with her empathy and resilience. Her journey shows how confronting life's hardships with courage can lead to a life of purpose and positive impact.

2. Steve Jobs: Reinvention After Setbacks

Steve Jobs' story is one of reinvention. After being forced out of Apple, the company he co-founded, Jobs could have viewed this as a failure. Instead, he saw it as an opportunity to grow, founding NeXT and acquiring Pixar. When he returned to Apple, he brought a renewed vision that transformed the company. His journey reminds us that setbacks are often the stepping stones to our most significant achievements.

3. Malala Yousafzai: Turning Adversity into Advocacy

Malala Yousafzai's life changed after she survived a Taliban attack for advocating girls' education. Rather than retreat, she found renewed strength and became a global voice for education and women's rights. Her story demonstrates how even the most difficult challenges fuel a powerful purpose impacting millions.

Embracing Your Destiny Transition

Every challenge in a destiny transition is an invitation to grow more robust, precise, and purposeful. These transitions test us in ways few experiences can, asking us to release old attachments and build resilience and trust in a path that may feel uncertain. But each step strengthens your faith and brings you closer to your calling.

As you move through your journey, know that you are not alone. Countless others have walked similar paths and emerged transformed, ready to make a difference. Embrace your transition, let it refine you, and remember that every obstacle overcome and every lesson learned prepares you for a future aligned with your highest purpose.

Destiny transitions are gifts, enabling us to live a life deeply aligned with our true calling. Embrace each challenge, fuel your faith, and trust that every moment leads you towards the life you are meant to live.

4

Staged Transitions:
Recognising the False Path

Life is a series of transitions, each marking a new stage in our journey. These transitions often bring both challenges and opportunities for growth. However, one of the most profound lessons I have learned is that not every transition leads us to our true destination. Sometimes, even with our best intentions and efforts, we find ourselves on a path that doesn't align with who we indeed are. This chapter explores the idea of "Staged Transitions," when it may seem that everything should fall into place, yet something feels fundamentally wrong.

I learned this lesson firsthand by observing the life and eventual passing of my father. His journey was marked by resilience, hard work, and perseverance, a testament to the human spirit's ability to push forward in the face of hardship and trouble. However, as much as he strived and gave of himself, his path didn't lead him to the victory he had hoped for. Watching him go through this taught me a powerful, albeit painful, truth: sometimes, no matter how hard we try, the path we walk at times may not be meant for us.

My father was a man of unwavering commitment, believing dedication would bring fulfilment. He worked tirelessly, striving to build a life of stability and success for his family. But as I watched him struggle, year after year, it became clear that each step seemed to require more from him without bringing him closer to peace or satisfaction. There was a disconnect, a sense that his destination always lay beyond reach, no matter how hard he pushed.

As he grew older, his journey revealed a painful irony: his pursuit of success and security became the very thing that weighed him down. My father's life was a series of transitions that, rather than bringing him closer to his true calling, seemed to pull him away. It was as if he was walking a path that was shaped by the expectations of others, by societal standards and obligations, rather than his purpose. He was climbing a ladder that leaned against the wrong wall, pursuing a victory that wasn't aligned with his deepest values.

Reflecting on his story, I understood that "Staged Transitions" are a universal part of the human experience. They are those critical moments when we must decide if the road we are travelling is our own. It is easy to become so focused on moving forward, proving ourselves, and achieving our goals that we lose sight of whether these goals are ours to pursue. The transition periods in life often bring us to a crossroads, and sometimes, they require us to pause and ask: "Am I on the right path?"

My father's struggles taught me that life has a way of placing obstacles not merely to challenge us but to awaken us. These barriers can act as signals, nudging us to reassess our choices and reflect on our direction. Unfortunately, many of us see obstacles only as things to overcome. We believe that the mere act of persevering is required to achieve fulfilment. But sometimes, obstacles are there to help us realise that we are pursuing something that doesn't resonate with our true purpose.

I learned that there is a difference between the struggle that builds us up and the struggle that wears us down. My father's journey was one of endless striving but lacked alignment. He never felt the satisfaction or inner peace from pursuing a path rooted in one's true purpose. This taught me that we must be vigilant about the direction in which we are moving. Otherwise, we risk spending our lives on a path that, while outwardly admirable, leaves us inwardly unfulfilled.

Staged Transitions are often disguised as failures or setbacks, but they are opportunities to recalibrate. They invite us to dig deeper and ask ourselves tough questions. Are we pursuing success as defined by others, or are we seeking a life that aligns with our core values? Are we moving forward out of habit and obligation, or does a true sense of purpose drive us?

When we find ourselves on a path that drains us rather than energises us, it may be a sign to pivot, reassess, and perhaps let go of the false path we have been on. This is the essence of recognising Staged Transitions: the willingness to pause, reflect, and choose a path that honours our unique purpose.

Though shaped by struggle, my father's legacy became a beacon for me and a reminder that life's most important transitions are not just about moving forward but about moving forward with intention. He showed me the importance of aligning our journey with our innermost truth, even if that means stepping away from what is familiar or accepted.

Today, I carry forward his memory not as a cautionary tale but as an invitation to live with courage and clarity, to listen to the whispers of life's transitions, and to recognise when a change in direction may lead to a more profound sense of fulfilment. May this chapter serve as a reminder that true success is not defined by the world's standards but by the peace that comes from knowing we are on the right path.

In honouring my father's life, I am reminded that sometimes, the most courageous choice is not to push forward but to pivot. We must recognise when a stage of life has run its course and let go of paths that no longer serve us. There will come a time for each of us to ask if we are on a path that aligns with our deepest values. And if the answer is no, let us find the courage to seek a path that does.

In his passing, my father left me with a profound legacy, the knowledge that life's true purpose is not in the relentless pursuit of goals imposed by others but in the quiet, courageous alignment with our inner truth. Though marked by struggle, his journey illuminated a fact for me: that life's transitions are not just about moving forward but about moving forward in the right direction.

His story isn't unique. Even organisations and pioneers who dared to break moulds have faced similar staged transitions. A powerful example is Nikola Tesla, the brilliant inventor and engineer who played a pivotal role in developing alternating current (AC) electricity. Tesla possessed a vision for technological advancement that could change the world. However, he encountered numerous staged transitions, setbacks, and missed opportunities that ultimately hindered his legacy and kept him from achieving full recognition in his lifetime.

Tesla was known for his groundbreaking work and far-reaching ideas, but he encountered financial, relational, and personal barriers throughout his career. After coming to the United States and working briefly with Thomas Edison, Tesla parted ways due to their differing approaches to electrical power (AC vs. DC) and a disagreement over payment. This split began a pattern where Tesla's unconventional ideas often clashed with his peers' and investors' commercially driven interests.

One of the most significant staged transitions in Tesla's life was his ambitious project, the Wardenclyffe Tower, designed to provide free wireless electricity to the world. Despite the potential of this invention, he struggled to secure funding and eventually lost support from his primary investor, J.P. Morgan. Without the resources to complete the project, Tesla's vision of a revolutionary wireless power system remained unrealised, and he ultimately abandoned it. This setback, a series of failed ventures, and declining health led him into relative obscurity and poverty.

Tesla's story highlights how staged transitions, missed funding opportunities, unfulfilled projects, and strained relationships—can disrupt even the most promising path to destiny. His life is a reminder that, while talent and vision are essential, successfully navigating transitions is often necessary to achieve one's purpose and impact.

The world often focuses on the few who overcome these struggles, leaving out the many who fall short. We hear about the two out of ten who succeed, but we rarely delve into the stories of the eight who didn't. We don't examine what went wrong during their transitions or why they couldn't overcome the struggles. Recognising these untold stories to mourn their loss and learn from their failures ensures that others don't repeat the same mistakes.

This is why, in some countries, the government protects children from abuse or neglect by their parents. They understand the power of these transitions. They know that a child's future is developed by the environment they grow up in. Unfortunately, I was raised in a society where parents' actions were rarely questioned. In such a society, children often walk the path laid out by their parents, even if it's destructive. The consequences of this can be seen in many people's lives today, who were shaped by mentors who may not have been equipped to guide them positively.

We must recognise that not all transitions are equal as we move forward. Some are designed to lead us to greatness, while others are set up to trap us. We must be vigilant, aware of the subtle forces at play, and consistently seek to understand the full scope of our challenges. Only then can we hope to reach our destiny and avoid the pitfalls of the "Staged Transition."

In honouring the legacies of those lost to such transitions, may we be inspired to rise above them, paving a more straightforward, brighter path for those who follow.

The concept of "Staged Transitions" as obstacles to one's destiny is a compelling framework highlighting the deceptive nature of confident life choices or external influences that can seem progressive but ultimately delay or derail personal growth. Let us explore each of these ideas and characteristics, as well as the spiritual dimensions, which bring a deeper level of understanding to the challenges people face on their journey to purpose.

Characteristics of Staged Transitions That Delay Destiny

1. **False Promises of Success:** Often, these misleading opportunities present themselves as significant breakthroughs but ultimately fall short. They consume time and resources without contributing to meaningful progress. Identifying these requires clarity on what truly aligns with one's core values and long-term vision.

2. **Detours That Consume Energy:** Staged transitions may act as detours, diverting attention from meaningful goals and draining resources. This is a common experience where people engage in tasks or roles that seem necessary but don't contribute to their higher purpose.

3. **Dependency on Unreliable Allies:** Sometimes, partnerships that appear supportive can be detrimental, as unreliable allies may hinder growth or cause setbacks. Developing discernment in identifying truly supportive relationships is crucial.

4. **Fear-Based Decisions:** Decisions made from fear rather than confidence can hold progress back. Many experience fear-driven choices, often leading to temporary comfort but may prevent alignment with their true path.

5. **Patterns of Stagnation:** Some transitions offer growth but lead to stagnation. Identifying these requires self-awareness and commitment to continuous development, especially when little advancement exists.

Familiar Sources of Staged Transitions

1. **Society and Cultural Norms:** Cultural expectations and societal pressures often push individuals to follow paths that may not align with their inner calling. For example, the expectation of pursuing financially lucrative careers can overshadow personal aspirations. Oprah Winfrey's story shows how pursuing a unique vision can counter societal pressures.

2. **Family Expectations and Traditions:** Family dynamics can influence life paths, especially in cultures with solid expectations. Elon Musk's decision to leave South Africa to pursue his goals in the U.S. exemplifies the courage it takes to honour personal vision over familial expectations.

3. **Economic Constraints:** Financial limitations can sometimes create staged transitions, where practicality leads people to settle rather than pursue their dreams. J.K. Rowling's story exemplifies resilience amid economic struggles and the importance of commitment to long-term goals.

4. **Government Policies and Systems:** Restrictive or systemic limitations can inhibit growth and freedom. Malala Yousafzai's fight for education rights amidst oppressive policies shows the impact of resilience against systemic obstacles.

5. **Cultural and Religious Values:** While cultural and religious beliefs can be guiding forces, they can also restrict individuals from exploring new paths that resonate with them. Galileo Galilei's story illustrates the courage needed to pursue knowledge despite opposition.

6. 6. **Spiritual Forces and Inner Struggles:** Belief in spiritual forces or internal battles often creates barriers to destiny. Frida Kahlo's journey of transforming inner turmoil into art showcases how confronting spiritual and emotional struggles can lead to profound personal growth.

Spiritual Aspect: Distractions and Negative Influences

1. **Internal Distractions:** Fear, insecurity, or unresolved past traumas can hinder progress. Nelson Mandela's journey highlights the importance of overcoming internal distractions to achieve a more excellent vision for humanity.

2. **External Negative Influences:** Discouraging people or cultural biases can subtly derail focus and drive. Malcolm X's resilience against societal biases showcases the power of rising above negativity.

3. **Spiritual Warfare and Faith:** Many cultures view spiritual warfare as a real force against individual destiny. The biblical story of Job demonstrates faith's role in overcoming trials and spiritual distractions.

By understanding these characteristics, sources, and spiritual aspects, individuals can make more conscious decisions that align with their purpose. This awareness fosters resilience against distractions and negative influences, paving the way for a life aligned with one's true destiny.

Breaking the Chains: How Generational Yokes and Patterns Shape "Staged Transitions"

This chapter felt complete until an unforgettable thought struck me, a reflection too profound to ignore. It happened one Saturday evening while watching Seven Doors, a Nollywood movie on Netflix by Femi Adebayo, with my wife. The film vividly explores the devastating grip of generational curses and patterns, illustrating how they can shape and bind the destinies of individuals and entire lineages.

In the story, a past-generation king, driven by greed and an insatiable hunger for power, sacrificed his seven wives to secure a longer reign on the throne. As a result, he lived an astonishing 170 years, but his prolonged rule came at a great cost. His selfish actions disrupted the natural order, depriving others destined for kingship of their opportunity to ascend the throne. His greed altered their paths and futures, creating a cycle of inherited struggles.

The new king, burdened by the weight of these past misdeeds, faced relentless trials to reclaim peace for himself and his people. To break free from the chains of these generational yokes, he underwent rigorous traditional rites and daunting tasks. The journey to liberation was far from easy, he paid a heavy price, including the ultimate sacrifice of his innocent daughter. Only then did he finally secure lasting peace for his kingdom.

Generational yokes are powerful forces that, while often invisible, can have a profound impact on our lives. My father once advised me to avoid following in his footsteps, encouraging me to carve out a unique life free from the struggles he faced. His words became my guiding principle. However, it wasn't until I encountered repeated patterns of hardship that closely resembled his that I began to understand the grip of generational cycles on my own life. These struggles often appear uninvited, sabotaging our progress and trapping us in a narrative written long before our time.

The Power of Recognition

Acknowledging the existence of generational yokes is the first step toward breaking free. Many people dismiss these forces, labeling their repeated misfortunes as bad luck. Yet, when you scrutinize the patterns, you'll see that some struggles are more inherited than accidental.

In my journey, I wrote down every habit, behavior, and limitation I noticed in my father's life that mirrored challenges in my own. This exercise became my battle plan for breaking the cycle. It wasn't easy choosing a new path never is. It meant letting go of relationships and habits that tied me to a repetitive loop of struggle. But if I could rewrite my narrative, so can you.

Lessons from the Rubenites, Jabez, and Noah's Children

The Rubenites' story in the Bible epitomizes the cost of generational yokes. Reuben, Jacob's firstborn, was cursed for his indiscretion, and his descendants bore the weight of this yoke. Despite being positioned for greatness, they struggled to claim their inheritance because of the sins of their forefather. The Rubenites teach us that unaddressed generational patterns can rob us of our potential, leaving us trapped in cycles of defeat.

Jabez, on the other hand, offers hope. Born into a lineage marked by pain, his very name meant sorrow. Yet, through wisdom and fervent prayer, Jabez cried out to God to break the chain of pain over his life. His boldness to seek a different destiny brought him blessings and expanded his territory, proving that generational yokes can be overcome with intentional action and faith.

Similarly, the children of Noah faced a different kind of generational yoke. Ham's dishonorable act toward his father led to a curse upon his lineage. His descendants endured hardships that could have been avoided had wisdom prevailed. This story highlights how parental patterns, even momentary decisions, can cast long shadows over future generations.

The Call to Break Free

Generational yokes are not unchangeable; rather, they are challenges meant to be overcome. Whether it's through the wisdom of God, the boldness and prayers of Jabez, or the strategic planning in my own life, breaking free from these inherited struggles requires awareness, intentionality, and perseverance.

Take a moment to reflect on your life. Are there patterns of failure, fear, or limitation that reflect your family's struggles? Breaking this chain may require sacrifices, tough decisions, and a steadfast commitment to change. However, the rewards are immense: a life unburdened, a fully realized destiny, and a legacy transformed for generations to come.

To overcome the challenges you face, I encourage you to rewrite your story. Your future, along with that of future generations, depends on your bravery to break free from these limitations. Remember, this is not just about you; it's about creating a powerful ripple effect of freedom, hope, and purpose for those who will follow in your footsteps.

$*5*$

External Forces that Influence Staged Transitions

Imagine growing up in a world where moral principles are reversed—where wrongdoing is celebrated as the shortcut to success. A place where love often disguises selfish motives, people disappear mysteriously, and society looks the other way. In such an environment, hatred is freely expressed, and fulfilling your destiny demands relentless spiritual battles. I have seen places where people's destinies are swapped or stolen, leaving their rightful owners in despair. This might sound surreal for many, but it was my reality: a place rich in potential, yet one where many great stars are dimmed before they can shine.

If not for the unique potential I carried and God's grace, I wouldn't be here to share my story. Each chapter of my life has been marked by transitions, overcoming spiritual attacks, pursuing education despite numerous challenges, and finding purpose amid chaos. These experiences, though daunting, have equipped me with strategies to turn adversity into opportunity, lessons I now share to inspire others.

A Birthday Celebration Gone Awry

One such lesson came unexpectedly during my daughter's ninth birthday. She was overjoyed and insisted on celebrating it with her classmates at school. Since her birthday fell on a weekday, we granted her a wish. To make it memorable, we hired a gift company to prepare parcels for her classmates, including a beautifully decorated cake. Everything was delivered to her school that morning, and we felt confident she would have a day to remember.

But by noon, the unexpected happened. My wife received a call from my daughter's class teacher. Apologising profusely, the teacher explained that the school had recently enforced a strict policy: consumable items, like cakes and snacks, were no longer allowed during birthday celebrations. Only non-consumable gifts could be distributed to the students.

At first, the reason seemed baffling. But the teacher revealed a disturbing backstory. She explained that some parents in the community had been exploiting their children's birthdays for sinister purposes. According to reports, these parents performed rituals over consumable items—cakes, drinks, biscuits, and so on—before sending them to school. Once the children consumed these items, their spiritual essence or "glory" would allegedly be transferred to the celebrant, leaving the other children spiritually barren.

Even more unsettling were cases where such rituals were used to initiate unsuspecting children into witchcraft. The teacher recounted a nearby school that had to shut down after a parent confessed to engaging in such practices, resulting in irreparable harm to the students. This revelation led many schools in the area, including my daughter's, to ban edible items at birthday celebrations for the safety of the children.

Hearing this left us speechless. It was hard to believe, yet the stories seemed undeniable. We agreed to the teacher's request to return the consumable items and only share the non-consumable ones with my daughter's classmates.

Unseen Battles in a Tangible World

That experience opened our eyes to the reality of spiritual battles. Innocent children and unsuspecting people often become victims of unseen forces. It is heartbreaking to imagine how a child could unknowingly lose their potential, only to grow up facing endless troubles despite hard work and dedication.

How can anyone thrive in a society where such practices persist? When someone steals the potential of 30 children in one act, it leaves those children struggling through life, unable to understand the invisible chains holding them back.

This situation serves as a sobering reminder that the world we see is not all there is. Spiritual vigilance and strength are essential to navigating these hidden challenges. We must stay alert, protect our families, and seek divine guidance through prayer and faith.

Breaking Free from Spiritual Bondage

Take, for instance, the story of a young woman, the last of 13 children in a polygamous family. Adored as her father's "good luck charm," her life appeared privileged. Yet beneath the surface, her birth was tied to a secret covenant that bound her success to her father's wealth. This arrangement ensured she could never marry or build her own life without his consent.

Despite the material care she received, her life was a gilded cage. Every attempt at a relationship ended in heartbreak, sabotaged by the invisible forces tying her to her father's prosperity. Years of frustration and confusion finally led her to a breaking point.

Through unwavering faith, relentless prayer, and a courageous decision to separate from her family, she broke free from the spiritual bondage that had controlled her life. It wasn't easy, but her resilience paid off. Today, she is happily married, raising a family, and living a life of triumph. Her story is a powerful testament to the strength to overcome unseen forces and reclaim your destiny.

At ten, my father, a skilled chess grandmaster, taught me and my siblings chess. I developed a passion for the game, competing nationally and gaining recognition. My peers would call me "Chess Boy," and I dreamt of becoming the first Nigerian world chess champion. Yet, over time, uncontrollable shaking overtook me before competitions, robbing me of focus and forcing me to quit. Despite my father's support, this unexplained force, what we would later understand as a spiritual attack, derailed my dreams. Losing recognition, my passion faded, and I eventually abandoned the game.

Reflecting now, I see how these struggles shaped my journey. While many battles in life can be fought with resilience and strategy, invisible battles that lie beyond our control present a unique challenge. In societies like mine, spiritual struggles are a reality we navigate alongside other barriers.

Overcoming visible struggles is challenging but manageable. People can find a way forward with perseverance, planning, grit, and self-discipline. But how do we handle struggles that we cannot see, define, or plan for? This is where the unseen challenges come in—the battles that are often invisible but just as accurate. In many African societies, faith and prayer play a central role because sometimes, people fight unseen battles that test the very essence of their destiny.

I once wrote that leaders in developed nations owe respect to those in underdeveloped countries because their environments enable leadership growth. In a country like the one I come from, we're often tasked with creating that environment ourselves, building our paths through systemic barriers. Had I grown up with empowering policies, a vibrant economy, or solid cultural support, I might have achieved my vision much sooner.

I am confident these unseen struggles have silenced many who couldn't share their stories. I recall a verse from Proverbs 29:2: *"When the righteous are in authority, the people rejoice: but when the wicked rule, the people mourn."* So many with potential have been left to suffer quietly while those who take darker paths seem to flourish. For those whose dreams have been shattered by invisible barriers and those still fighting against them, I share my story to stand with you, inspire resilience, and offer hope.

Economic and Social Pressures as Sources of Distraction

Financial pressures can become powerful distractions in societies facing economic challenges, often pulling people away from their proper paths. Aspirations can take a back seat when basic survival is a daily struggle. Many people in under-resourced communities must prioritise immediate needs over long-term goals. This environment can delay dreams, as financial constraints overshadow ambitions and push individuals into survival rather than growth mode.

Social pressures add another layer, as communities sometimes impose limiting beliefs and expectations. Instead of pursuing their passions, many young people feel compelled to settle into traditional roles or follow societal norms to avoid criticism. These pressures can cloud one's vision, turning life into a series of concessions rather than fulfilling transitions.

How Family, Friends, and Societal Expectations Influence Transitions

Family and friends can be a source of encouragement or a barrier, shaping how one perceives their potential. Sometimes, families may impose their expectations, consciously or unconsciously, leading individuals away from their authentic path. Friends, too, can sway choices; their successes or failures create benchmarks that inspire or inhibit progress.

Societal expectations often reinforce these influences. The pressure to "fit in" can stifle unique aspirations in communities where conformity is valued over individuality. Following these influences without self-reflection can lead people down paths that feel disconnected from their true selves, making transitions feel less like growth and more like giving in to external demands.

Identifying When a Transition is Forced Rather than Authentic.

Knowing when a transition is forced rather than authentic is crucial to finding fulfilment. Authentic transitions feel challenging yet rewarding, aligned with personal values and a sense of purpose. On the other hand, forced transitions often bring a lingering dissatisfaction and lack of motivation, as they are usually responses to external pressures rather than internal goals. However, learning to identify these differences involves self-awareness and honesty. When deciding, ask: "Is this what I want," or "Am I doing this to meet someone else's expectations?" Cultivating the habit of self-reflection can protect us from paths that don't align with our true potential.

In conclusion, life's journey unfolds through stages that shape and redefine us. While some transitions align naturally with our growth, others feel imposed, challenging us to find strength and purpose within. Remember that you're not alone if you face invisible barriers or feel diverted from your dreams. Like the story of the young woman breaking free from her father's covenant, my journey reminds me that resilience is born in the darkest times, and our purpose becomes most apparent when we are determined to rise, no matter the circumstance.

6

Overcoming Staged Transitions

In the previous chapter, we explored how visible transitions can be challenging but manageable, while the hidden forces that subtly shape our lives often strike without warning. These staged transitions have a unique power to separate us from our true purpose. Reconnecting with that purpose afterwards can feel almost impossible, as if finding our way back through a maze we never saw coming. However, while optimism is valuable and keeps us hopeful during hard times, when life's invisible forces strike, optimism alone isn't always enough. These challenges don't discriminate; they come to everyone, regardless of mindset or status. True strength isn't about being positive all the time. It is about showing grit: the courage to keep going, even when optimism fades.

But how do we overcome these hidden forces that threaten to pull us off course? One powerful approach is to learn from those who have faced and conquered similar challenges. Leaders like Nelson Mandela, Dr. Ben Carson, and Curtis Jackson (50 Cent) encountered incredible obstacles that could have crushed their potential. Instead, their journeys provide a blueprint for building resilience and overcoming the unseen barriers life can throw in our path. Their stories inspire us to face each challenge with determination and remind us that, with persistent courage, we can survive and thrive.

Many individuals also face hidden spiritual or societal forces that shape their outcomes. For example, a Pew Research study found that 62% of Americans identify as spiritual or religious, with many believing that unseen forces influence their destiny. In Nigeria, 58% of respondents in a Gallup study attributed significant life events to spiritual factors. These beliefs reflect how unseen spiritual, psychological, or societal forces can become barriers that either motivate perseverance or create passivity. By acknowledging these forces and seeking paths to reconnect with our true purpose, we can build the resilience to overcome even the most invisible challenges.

Understanding and Overcoming "Staged Transitions" Through Migration

Life's greatest transformations often demand a physical shift, a migration from one environment to another. Whether these transitions are caused by economic hardship, spiritual callings, or personal ambitions, the act of moving can unlock the potential to overcome challenges that seem insurmountable in your current circumstances. To remain stagnant in a society that limits your growth often minimizes your efficiency, whereas relocating can amplify your effectiveness and open doors to opportunity.

Consider the story of Prophet Muhammad (PBUH). When faced with relentless persecution in Mecca, he was forced to migrate to Medina a monumental "staged transition" in Islamic history. This journey, known as the Hijra, was not just a physical migration but a transformational moment that redefined his mission. In Medina, Muhammad (PBUH) found a supportive community, established governance based on unity and justice, and laid the foundation for the spread of Islam. His migration teaches us that sometimes, leaving a hostile environment is essential for fulfilling one's purpose and building something greater.

Similarly, the biblical story of David offers another profound example. When King Saul sought to kill him out of jealousy, David had no choice but to flee. His migration from Saul's court into the wilderness was not a retreat but a strategy for survival and growth. During his time in exile, David built alliances, strengthened his leadership, and deepened his faith in God. This period of transition prepared him for his eventual role as king, showcasing that adversity and migration often serve as stepping stones to greatness.

In more recent times, Elon Musk's migration journey provides a modern-day example of overcoming staged transitions. Born in South Africa, Musk faced limitations to his dreams due to the lack of resources and opportunities in his home country. His move to North America, first to Canada and later to the United States, allowed him to immerse himself in an environment ripe for innovation. By migrating, Musk accessed the tools, networks, and opportunities that enabled him to build groundbreaking companies like Tesla, SpaceX, and Neuralink. His journey demonstrates how strategic relocation can transform challenges into achievements.

Even on a broader scale, economic hardship often forces individuals to migrate for survival and growth. For instance, during periods of inflation or political instability, skilled professionals like doctors and engineers often move to more developed countries to escape economic constraints. These migrations, though challenging, can shift individuals from being victims of flawed systems to victors in thriving economies. However, it is critical to ensure that such migrations are driven by purpose and not by mere influence or imitation. Those who migrate without clarity may find regret instead of renewal.

Migration, when aligned with purpose and understanding, is not just an escape, it is a transformative leap. Like Isaac, who moved to the land of Gerar during famine and turned adversity into prosperity, every great transition holds the potential for growth. Isaac's decision to sow in a land struck by famine exemplifies the power of resilience, adaptability, and faith during transitions. He transformed scarcity into abundance, proving that migration, when guided by purpose, can lead to unparalleled success.

However, life most profound transitions often require leaving behind the familiar to embrace the unknown. Whether you are navigating spiritual growth, economic hardship, or personal ambition, remember this: migration is not the end of one chapter but the beginning of a new one. It is a bridge from limitation to possibility, from hardship to triumph. Just like Muhammad (PBUH), David, and Musk, your willingness to embrace migration can lead to breakthroughs that reshape not just your life but the world around you.

So, when life presents you with a staged transition, ask yourself: will you stay in a place that limits your potential, or will you take the bold step to migrate toward your destiny? The choice to move physically, mentally, or spiritually can transform challenges into opportunities and lead you to the greatness that awaits.

Real-Life Examples of People Who Escaped Negative Cycles

Beyond famous figures, many individuals have found ways to escape negative cycles imposed by their environment or circumstances. These stories remind us that transformation is always possible. For instance, individuals who grew up in impoverished neighbourhoods but became business leaders or overcame systemic educational challenges are proof of what is achievable. Their stories show that anyone can defy their environment and create a positive future by embracing resilience and purpose.

Nelson Mandela: Triumph Over Injustice

Nelson Mandela's journey is one of history's most remarkable stories of resilience. Born in apartheid-era South Africa, Mandela grew up witnessing racial discrimination that dehumanised most of the population. As a young lawyer and activist, he joined the African National Congress (ANC) and dedicated himself to dismantling apartheid through peaceful protests.

However, his commitment came at a significant cost. In 1962, Mandela was arrested and later sentenced to life imprisonment for his efforts to overthrow the apartheid regime. For 27 years, he endured harsh conditions in prison, separated from his family and the cause he fought for. Yet, rather than allowing bitterness or despair to consume him, Mandela used his imprisonment to reflect, learn, and refine his vision for a united South Africa.

Released in 1990, Mandela quickly became a symbol of reconciliation, advocating for forgiveness instead of revenge. His leadership played a pivotal role in South Africa's transition to democracy, and in 1994, he became the country's first Black president. Mandela's life teaches us that perseverance and a commitment to higher ideals can lead to transformative change, even in the face of overwhelming injustice.

Dr. Ben Carson: Overcoming Poverty with Education and Faith

Dr. Ben Carson's story exemplifies the power of determination, education, and faith. Born into poverty in Detroit, Michigan, Carson faced significant challenges, including being raised by a single mother who could barely read. Struggling academically and plagued by a violent temper, he seemed destined for failure. However, his mother, Sonya Carson, believed in the power of education and encouraged her sons to read two weekly library books, summarising them for her. This routine transformed Carson's life. He loved learning, particularly in science, and his grades improved dramatically.

Carson's academic success led him to Yale University and later to the University of Michigan Medical School. Despite racism and self-doubt, he excelled and eventually became one of the world's most renowned neurosurgeons. In 1987, Carson made history by performing the first successful separation of conjoined twins at the back of the head.

His story is a testament to the belief that one's background does not determine their destiny. Through perseverance, faith, and hard work, Carson rose above adversity to become a symbol of hope and possibility.

Curtis Jackson (50 Cent): Turning Adversity into Opportunity

Curtis Jackson, famously known as 50 Cent, grew up in Queens, New York, during a time of economic hardship and widespread violence. Orphaned at eight after his mother's death and his father's absence, Jackson was raised by his grandparents in a rough neighbourhood.

At a young age, he became involved in drug dealing, a path fraught with danger and instability. By his late teens, Jackson had been arrested multiple times and faced near-death experiences, including being shot nine times in 2000. Surviving this brutal attack marked a turning point in his life.

Determined to leave behind his past, Jackson poured his energy into music. He honed his skills as a rapper and songwriter, using his life experiences as raw material for his art. His debut album, *Get Rich or Die Tryin'*, became a massive success, launching him into international stardom.

Beyond music, Jackson expanded his career into business, acting, and entrepreneurship, building a diverse portfolio that includes investments in fashion, beverages, and entertainment. His resilience, adaptability, and ability to turn setbacks into opportunities demonstrate the power of reinvention.

Finding Your Resilience

These stories remind us that life's hidden challenges aren't the end—they are an opportunity to grow stronger. Every setback has a lesson, and every struggle can shape us into something more significant.

When optimism isn't enough, let determination take over. Look to those who have walked similar paths and draw strength from their example. Life's most challenging transitions can't define you unless you let them. With grit, courage, and a clear sense of purpose, you can overcome anything and emerge even more robust.

A Simple Blueprint for Resilience

1. **Recognise the Challenge:** Don't ignore the forces affecting you; face them head-on.
2. **Learn from Others:** Find inspiration in the stories of those who have overcome similar struggles.
3. **Focus on Growth:** Use challenges as opportunities to learn and evolve.
4. **Keep Moving Forward:** When hope falters, rely on grit to carry you through.
5. **Reconnect with Purpose:** Stay rooted in your goals and values.

Life's hidden forces might knock you off course, but they can't stop you. With perseverance, you can survive, thrive, and leave behind a story of resilience and triumph.

One unforgettable story of resilience involves a woman I recently met whose journey profoundly changed my perspective on perseverance. She was a deeply devoted Christian, active in her church, and full of purpose. Her life reflected her faith, love, family, and community values. She married a man she believed shared her vision, but her reality unravelled painfully over time.

Her husband, who once appeared loving and supportive, became abusive. Despite her prayers, efforts, and belief in the sanctity of marriage, their union dissolved in a bitter divorce. As devastating as the breakup was, what followed shook her even more. Seeking solace from her church family, she found betrayal instead. The community she relied on for spiritual guidance harboured individuals whose actions were damaging rather than supportive. This betrayal left her heartbroken and questioning her faith and sense of belonging. With her sense of purpose shattered, she faced the overwhelming challenge of raising a child alone. Financial hardships mounted, forcing her to make decisions she had never imagined. Desperate to provide for her child, she found herself working as a sex worker, a path she never envisioned and one that felt worlds away from the life she once knew.

This was not a life of choice but one of survival, a reflection of how cruel circumstances can force people into places they never thought they would go. Yet, even amid this struggle, her resilience shone through. She never stopped prioritising her child's well-being and never abandoned the hope of reclaiming a better future.

Her journey taught me resilience is not a perfect, linear march towards success. It is messy, filled with heartbreak and moments of questioning one's worth. It is about surviving the days when the world is against you and finding the courage to hold onto even the faintest glimmer of hope.

Her story reminded me of the hidden battles so many face. Like Nelson Mandela, Dr. Ben Carson, or Curtis Jackson (50 Cent), her journey reflects the human spirit's capacity to endure and persevere. She may not yet be living her dream life, but her strength in facing unimaginable challenges is a testament to resilience. It is a powerful reminder that life's transitions—no matter how staged or unexpected—do not define us. It is how we respond to them that shapes our legacy.

Strategies for Breaking Free from Imposed Transitions

Breaking free from imposed transitions requires resilience and a proactive approach to shaping your environment. Mandela found strength through discipline and his vision for equality, while Carson focused intensely on education to escape the limits of poverty. These examples remind us to pursue what empowers us, even if society or circumstance tries to hold us back. A consistent focus on our goals, combined with the courage to adapt, can turn even the harshest situations into opportunities for growth.

Building Self-Awareness to Discern True Direction

Self-awareness is a powerful tool for navigating transitions. Mandela's steadfast commitment to his beliefs gave him clarity, helping him resist distractions and remain focused on his goal of ending apartheid. Carson's focus on academics stemmed from a deep understanding of his potential. Self-awareness helps us recognise when external forces push us in directions that don't align with our true purpose. Developing this clarity allows us to navigate transitions with purpose, whether visible or unseen.

As we conclude this chapter, remember that life's staged transitions can be overwhelming. Yet, we have the power to choose our response. We can survive and thrive by learning from those who have walked this path, built self-awareness, and broken free of limiting cycles. Embrace your journey, for every challenge brings you closer to your desired destiny. Let the stories of others inspire you to face each transition with courage, resilience, and the certainty that your dreams are within reach.

7

Personal Destiny and Spiritual Influence

The impact of territorial spirits on individual destiny is often overlooked, yet their influence can be profound. From my experiences and observations, I have understood how these unseen forces can derail even the most capable and well-intentioned individuals. As they are often described, territorial spirits operate independently, regardless of one's qualifications, social standing, or aspirations. They are not moved by ambition but by two essential factors: power and wisdom—the power to resist their influence and the knowledge to navigate the circumstances they create.

These spiritual forces can manifest as barriers to productivity, creating unseen obstacles that hinder personal growth and fulfilment. Their presence is incredibly potent in societies where corruption, systemic flaws, and unethical values prevail, offering them fertile ground to thrive. Conversely, in societies with solid justice systems, ethical frameworks, and supportive social structures, the influence of these forces is minimised. This distinction highlights how environments shaped by moral decay can amplify spiritual challenges, further complicating the paths of even the most gifted individuals.

One powerful example of resilience against such forces is the story of David Yonggi Cho, the founder of the Yoido Full Gospel Church in South Korea. Significant spiritual battles marked Cho's journey as he worked to establish and expand his ministry. Early in his mission, he encountered what he described as territorial spirits, unseen forces actively resisting his efforts to bring spiritual transformation to his community. These challenges threatened to derail the impact of his ministry.

Recognising that traditional methods alone would not suffice, Cho turned to deep spiritual practices for strength. He organised regular prayer and fasting sessions, even establishing dedicated "prayer mountains" where his congregation gathered to seek divine intervention. These intense periods of spiritual focus became a cornerstone of his ministry's success, fortifying both Cho and his followers against the obstacles they faced. Through his unwavering faith and disciplined spiritual approach, Cho overcame these forces and empowered thousands to rise above the barriers in their own lives.

Cho's journey underscores an essential truth: while territorial spirits and unseen forces can hinder progress, they are not invincible. His story reminds us that faith, focus, and perseverance can overcome even the most daunting challenges. We are not powerless in the face of unseen forces. By embracing spiritual resilience and a disciplined approach, we can chart a path through the obstacles that threaten to separate us from our destiny.

This perspective calls us to action, encouraging us to evaluate the environments we inhabit and the values we uphold. We can create conditions limiting hostile forces' influence through systemic reform, ethical living, or personal spiritual practices. Ultimately, the power to reclaim our destiny lies in aligning our lives with truth, justice, and unwavering determination.

How People Navigate Personal Success Considering Spiritual Beliefs

Success often requires more than skill, strategy, and determination. It involves navigating spiritual realities that shape the environments we live and work in. For many, faith serves as both a shield and a compass, helping them overcome challenges that logic or effort alone cannot address. Success becomes a dynamic interplay of personal effort, spiritual discipline, and reliance on a higher power.

One compelling story of navigating personal success through spiritual beliefs comes from David Yonggi Cho, the founder of the Yoido Full Gospel Church in South Korea. In a post-war nation grappling with widespread poverty and uncertainty, Cho envisioned building a thriving ministry to transform lives. However, he soon encountered spiritual resistance, attributed to territorial spirits seeking to undermine his mission. Rather than succumbing to despair, Cho turned to relentless prayer and fasting. He established a "prayer mountain" where thousands gathered for spiritual renewal, turning their faith into a force of collective strength. His discipline and unwavering trust in God allowed him to overcome barriers and build one of the largest congregations in the world, inspiring millions to rise above their challenges.

Similarly, the Apostle Paul's teachings on "principalities and powers" resonate deeply with those navigating unseen obstacles. Paul urged believers to put on the "full armour of God" as a defence against spiritual forces. His metaphor speaks to the reality that success often requires confronting challenges beyond the physical—those forces attempting to block progress in mysterious and intangible ways.

A modern-day example of spiritual resilience in personal success is the story of Colonel Harland Sanders, the founder of KFC. By his 60s, Sanders had faced a series of failures: failed businesses, lost jobs, and multiple rejections as he attempted to franchise his chicken recipe. However, Sanders often spoke of how his faith in God kept him going. He believed his recipe was a God-given talent and clung to the promise that persistence would yield results.

At 65, after being turned down over a thousand times, Sanders finally secured his first successful franchise deal. His reliance on prayer and belief that his struggles were part of a divine plan gave him the strength to persist. His journey shows that spiritual beliefs can offer clarity and endurance in the face of overwhelming odds.

Whether through intense prayer and fasting, as in the case of David Yonggi Cho, or through unshakable faith and persistence, as demonstrated by Colonel Sanders, spiritual beliefs can be a powerful ally in navigating personal success. By leaning into faith, individuals often find the strength to overcome obstacles and a deeper sense of purpose in their efforts. Remember, success is not merely the result of your hard work; it is a product of alignment between your efforts, environment, and the spiritual forces around you. Let your faith guide and determination sustain you when challenges arise, and allow your vision to inspire you. In this balance, you will find the pathway to enduring success.

Stories of Individuals Who Overcame or Succumbed to Spiritual Challenges

1. John G. Lake and the Spiritual Climate of South Africa

John G. Lake, a renowned evangelist and missionary, faced extraordinary spiritual opposition during his ministry in South Africa in the early 20th century. The region's history of colonialism, racial oppression, and conflict had fostered what he described as a "spiritual climate" that seemed resistant to transformation. Lake believed these territorial spirits manifested as barriers to progress, both spiritually and socially.

Instead of retreating in the face of such adversity, Lake confronted these challenges head-on. He led intense prayer meetings, teaching followers to engage in spiritual warfare with strong faith. His dedication bore fruit as he established over 600 churches, transforming the region's spiritual landscape. Lake's success wasn't just about the number of churches but the ripple effect of his ministry, which inspired countless others to rise above their circumstances and claim their destinies. His legacy remains a powerful example of how persistence and reliance on divine strength can overcome even the most oppressive spiritual climates.

2. Brother Yun: The Heavenly Man

Brother Yun, a Chinese Christian leader and author of "The Heavenly Man," exemplifies resilience in the face of relentless spiritual and physical persecution. Growing up in a place deeply hostile to Christianity, Yun was subjected to repeated imprisonment, torture, and attempts to break his spirit.

Despite being starved, beaten, and left in isolation, Yun's faith never wavered. One of the most miraculous moments in his journey came when he escaped from a maximum-security prison. Guards were stationed at every exit, yet he walked out unnoticed, a feat Yun attributes to divine intervention. His story reveals that resilience is not merely about enduring hardships but about trusting in a higher power to provide a way out, even when escape seems impossible.

Yun's journey illustrates that spiritual strength can overcome external opposition and unseen forces. Though his path was filled with suffering, his unwavering faith became his shield, enabling him to rise above unimaginable challenges and inspire others to stand firm in their beliefs.

3. David Yonggi Cho: Resilience in South Korea

David Yonggi Cho, the founder of the Yoido Full Gospel Church, also faced intense spiritual resistance while establishing his ministry in South Korea. In a nation still grappling with the scars of war and cultural upheaval, Cho encountered territorial spirits that sought to undermine his efforts to bring hope and transformation to his community.

Recognising the need for spiritual discipline, Cho turned to prayer and fasting as his weapons of choice. His story is a testament to the power of faith and discipline in breaking through the unseen forces that seek to hinder progress.

Lessons from Their Stories

The journeys of John G. Lake, Brother Yun, and David Yonggi Cho are potent reminders that spiritual challenges, though daunting, can be overcome. These individuals faced overwhelming opposition, both seen and unseen, but refused to let their circumstances dictate their destinies. Their stories teach us that resilience is forged in the fires of faith, determination, and an unyielding commitment to one's purpose.

While the unseen forces of life may seek to derail us, they also provide opportunities for growth and transformation. Each obstacle becomes a stepping stone when met with courage and faith. Just as Lake confronted the spiritual climate of South Africa, Yun trusted divine protection in the face of persecution, and Cho fortified his ministry through prayer. We, too, can rise above the challenges that threaten to hold us back.

As you reflect on your life, remember this: no matter how formidable the opposition, you possess the power to overcome it. Each trial is a chance to deepen your resolve, strengthen your faith, and claim the destiny that is uniquely yours. The journey may not be easy, but it is always worth it. Let these stories inspire you to rise, persevere, and leave a legacy of strength, purpose, and unwavering hope.

Your destiny is within reach; embrace it with courage and determination.

❀8❀

Developing Faith and Resilience Through Transition

There was a time in my life when I used to think God didn't love me. I believed He was partial, unfair, and even cruel because life seemed to deal me the worst cards. While others my age were enjoying life's blessings, I was struggling to fight battles that felt insurmountable. To me, it looked as though they were more favoured, and I was left out. My heart grew bitter as I wrestled with these feelings and often questioned God's intentions.

There were moments during my darkest transitions when life felt so overwhelming that I just wanted God to let me die. The pain seemed endless, the struggles unrelenting. To make it worse, my enemies thrived while I suffered. I could see their joy and laughter as I fought through each day. I asked God, "Why can't You just destroy them? Why do they get to rejoice while I endure so much pain?"

It was a messy, heartbreaking situation I wouldn't wish on anyone. As I reflect, I know not everyone could survive such a storm. If ten people had to walk the same path, I doubt more than two would make it out alive. But I am here today to tell my story not as a victim but as a victor. My journey has turned into a testimony that inspires others.

I've said, "I've walked through the land of darkness and the land of light, but I chose the light because it's better to see than to live in blindness." That choice didn't come easy. Only through understanding and applying certain principles of faith could I prevail over my struggles.

Faith Changes Everything

When I surrendered to Christ, the world began to look different. The trials that once seemed like immovable mountains became stepping stones towards my purpose. A scripture that profoundly impacted me was Luke 10:19: *"I have given you authority to trample on snakes and scorpions and to overcome all the power of the enemy; nothing will harm you."*

This verse wasn't just comforting; it became a weapon of empowerment. It changed the way I saw my enemies and my struggles. Instead of viewing them with hatred or fear, I started recognising their role in my transformation.

Through faith, I began to see how every challenge refined me. My enemies thought they were hindering me, but they were instruments of God, pushing me to grow. Their actions drove me to my knees in prayer, where I discovered strength, resilience, and clarity. Today, I look back and thank them, for they unknowingly helped me find my purpose.

The Power of "Violent Faith"

Faith became my anchor, but it wasn't just passive belief. It was what I call "violent faith." This is the kind of bold, unwavering trust described in Matthew 17:20: *If you have faith as small as a mustard seed, you can say to this mountain, 'Move,' and it will move."*

Violent faith demands action. It requires perseverance in the face of adversity, declaring with confidence, "I will overcome, no matter what!" It's the kind of faith that challenges the impossible and dares to believe that better days are ahead.

This faith carried me through my toughest battles and revealed God's plan for my life. It reminded me that every struggle has a purpose, and every setback holds the potential for a comeback.

Faith and Purpose: A Divine Partnership

Faith and purpose are inseparable. Faith gives us the strength to face life's transitions, while purpose provides the direction that makes our struggles meaningful. Together, they create a foundation that sustains us in times of trial.

Take Joni Eareckson Tada, for example. After a diving accident left her paralysed at 17, Joni initially struggled with depression and anger. Yet, through faith, she discovered a higher purpose in her pain. Instead of succumbing to despair, she embraced her role as an advocate for others with disabilities. Her art, writing, and speaking inspired millions, proving that even the most challenging transitions can lead to profound impact when fueled by faith and purpose.

Similarly, Bethany Hamilton found her faith tested when she lost her arm to a shark attack at 13. For many, such an event could have signaled the end of a dream. But Bethany trusted that God had a plan for her life. Her faith gave her the resilience to get back on her surfboard and, later, to use her story to inspire others. Her purpose was to surf and show the world the power of perseverance and faith.

In the Bible, Job's story highlights this connection. Job's faith sustained him as he endured unimaginable losses, his children, wealth, and health. Yet, his unwavering trust in God's purpose for his life allowed him to persevere. Ultimately, his faith was rewarded, and his story continues to inspire countless people facing transitions.

Faith and purpose are like the wings of an eagle: they work together to lift us above our challenges and enable us to see life from a broader, more hopeful perspective.

Practical Exercises to Build Resilience

Building endurance, spiritually and mentally, is a process that requires intentionality. Here are practical exercises, coupled with inspiring stories, to strengthen your ability to navigate life's challenges:

1. **Daily Gratitude Practice:** Cultivate gratitude by journalling three things that you are thankful for each day. Gratitude shifts your focus from problems to possibilities. Nick Vujicic, born without arms or legs, practices gratitude as a core principle. Despite his physical limitations, Nick's faith in God and daily focus on what he can do instead of what he can't has enabled him to inspire millions worldwide.

2. **Immerse Yourself in Prayer and Meditation:** Set aside time daily for prayer or meditation to connect with God and clarify your purpose. Bethany Hamilton leaned heavily on prayer to find the strength to return to the ocean after her accident. In these moments of connection, she found the courage to pursue her calling, even with one arm.

3. **Study and Reflect on the Scripture:** Engage with scripture that speaks to perseverance, such as Hebrews 11, which recounts stories of faith overcoming adversity. For example, Job's story in the Bible teaches us to trust God even when life feels unfair. Reflecting on such stories can remind you that struggles are often stepping stones towards a more significant purpose.

4. **Seek Community and Accountability:** Surround yourself with people who encourage you and share your values. Joni Eareckson Tada's journey was strengthened by her supportive community of faith, which uplifted her and helped her find creative ways to express herself.

5. **Visualise Victory and Speak Positivity:** Visualise the outcomes you hope for and speak life into your situation. Nick Vujicic often speaks about the power of affirmations and visualising God's plan for his life. These practices reinforce resilience and fuel determination.

Your life is not defined by your struggles but by how you rise from them. Faith doesn't remove the storms, but it aids you through them. Each trial you face is a chapter in your testimony, a story that will inspire others and glorify God. As you navigate your transitions, remember: "You are not a victim of your circumstances. You are a vessel of God's purpose." Trust Him to use every hardship to refine you, every tear to cleanse you, and every victory to glorify Him.

This is not the end of your journey. It is the foundation for something extraordinary. Keep walking, keep believing, and watch as faith turns your pain into purpose and your trials into triumphs. Your best chapters are yet to be written.

Building a Support System for Destiny Transitions

One of life's deepest pains during transition seasons is navigating the journey without a support system. Whether it is due to an unsupportive society or the absence of people to uplift you, the path can feel unbearably lonely. Yet, what brings hope and relief during these transitions is the truth that divinely orchestrated destiny often provides the framework for the support you need if only you recognise and embrace it.

But what if you find yourself in a challenging environment like the one I grew up in? A society where every step forward seems tethered to the need for money, where even dreams come with a price tag and support is rarely offered without expectation. People often dismiss your aspirations in such places, doing nothing unless personal benefit is involved. Breaking through in such a world requires grit, resourcefulness, and an unwavering determination to persevere despite the odds.

I vividly recall my journey towards becoming an author, a dream that burned in my heart 15 years before I wrote my first book. Those years were riddled with rejection and financial struggles. I reached out to people, hoping for guidance or support, but their responses were often discouraging, leaving me disheartened but not defeated. I discovered that I needed to rely on my inner resilience and find a way to fund my dream independently.

Determined to press forward, I turned to freelancing, leveraging my natural talents to earn what little I could. With every job I completed, I inched closer to self-publishing my book. It was an uphill battle, made even more daunting by the harsh economic realities of my country. Yet, amidst those challenges, I found a strength I never knew I possessed. That strength, faith, and determination carried me through one of the most trying periods of my life. Today, as I reflect on that journey, I thank God I didn't give up. Each step, no matter how small, was part of a more excellent plan to shape my destiny.

Finding Mentors, Friends, and Resources That Support Growth

Building a support system starts with seeking out mentors, friends, and tools that align with your vision. It's not about waiting for the right people to appear—it's about positioning yourself to find them. Mentors offer wisdom to avoid pitfalls, friends remind you of your worth, and resources provide the tangible means to transform ideas into action.

Consider the story of Oprah Winfrey, who overcame extreme poverty, abuse, and rejection to become one of the most influential figures in the world. Early in her career, she encountered hinderances, but key mentors like Maya Angelou inspired her to find her voice and redefine her goals. Oprah also relied on self-education, reading extensively, and learning from the stories of others. These relationships and resources became the cornerstone of her success, reinforcing that no one thrives in isolation.

If you are stuck, ask yourself: "Who has the wisdom I need? What resources can I tap into? Who will celebrate my victories with me?" Surround yourself with people who fuel your growth, not those who diminish it. And don't forget to seek out communities—whether through social media, local groups, or professional networks that share your passion and purpose.

The Inspiring Journey of Afolabi Shittu: A Story of Perseverance and Destiny

Some stories move us, and others ignite a fire within us. The life of Afolabi Shittu is one of those rare narratives that remind us of the power of resilience and the beauty of embracing life's transitions. Afolabi's journey not only fills my heart with pride but also inspires me to see transitional phases as opportunities for growth.

I first met Afolabi in 2021 when I decided to take up boxing. He became my trainer, and as we spent time together, he opened up about his life story. I was struck by his determination and passion, qualities that shone through despite his incredible hardships. Moved by his dreams and unwavering spirit, I supported him financially and mentored him without hesitation. I believed sincerely in his potential; today, his story proves that belief in oneself can move mountains.

Afolabi's challenges began early. At just five years old, his parents separated, forcing his mother to move with him to a slum after losing the financial stability of city life. Life was a daily struggle, but even as a child, Afolabi carried something extraordinary within—a quiet fire that refused to be extinguished.

As he grew older, life tested him further. From working as a bus conductor to hawking goods on the streets, Afolabi's days were filled with challenges that would have defeated many. Yet, he persevered. He didn't just endure; he dreamed.

His life took an unexpected turn when his mother remarried, this time to a boxing coach. Seeing an opportunity, Afolabi joined his stepfather's team, channelling his pain and determination into the ring. What he began as a way of coping with life's struggles soon revealed itself as his calling. Through hard work and relentless practice, Afolabi became a champion in Lagos.

But his story doesn't stop there. One day, Afolabi's boxing skills caught the eye of a man from the United States on social media. Touched by his talent and inspired by his story, this man adopted Afolabi as his protégé, offering him support and guidance. This pivotal moment marked the start of a new chapter in Afolabi's life.

Today, Afolabi lives in the United Kingdom and boxes for one of the most prestigious clubs in the world. His journey from the slums of Lagos to the international stage is a testament to the power of perseverance, belief, and the ability to embrace transitional phases as stepping stones to greatness.

I firmly believe Afolabi will one day achieve his dream of becoming Africa's greatest boxer and earning worldwide recognition. His story reminds us that no matter where you start or how difficult the road may seem, the power to rise lies within.

How Positive Influences Reinforce Purpose

Positive influences are like a lighthouse during a storm. They guide you towards your destination, even when the path is unclear. These influences are not always loud or obvious; sometimes, they come in quiet acts of encouragement or unexpected opportunities.

A powerful example is that of Albert Einstein. As a young student, Einstein struggled in traditional schooling and often felt alienated by his peers. However, one teacher, Max Talmey, saw his potential and began lending him advanced books on mathematics and philosophy. This mentorship helped Einstein channel his curiosity into groundbreaking discoveries, reinforcing his belief in his purpose despite early struggles.

Your purpose becomes more apparent when the right people and influences surround you. It might be a teacher, friend, or even a stranger who offers encouragement. Embrace these moments. They are divine reminders that you are on the right track. And remember, positivity is contagious. As you benefit from others' influence, please pass it on to those who need it most.

Identifying and Distancing from Negative Influences

Learning to identify and step away from negative influences is just as important as finding positive influences. These could be people, environments, or habits that stifle your growth. Negativity is subtle, often disguised as "tough love" or hidden in the familiarity of relationships that no longer serve you.

One striking story is that of Sara Blakely, the founder of Spanx. Before launching her billion-dollar company, Blakely faced relentless scepticism from people around her. Many dismissed her idea as impractical, but she refused to let their negativity define her destiny. Instead, she limited her interactions with doubters and leaned into her belief in her vision. Her journey teaches us that walking away from negative voices often creates the space needed for progress.

Distancing yourself from negativity doesn't mean abandoning relationships entirely. It means prioritising your mental and emotional well-being. Reflect on the people and habits in your life. Are they propelling you forward or holding you back? Let go of what no longer serves you, and trust that making room for positivity will attract the support you need.

Transitions, though daunting, are also opportunities to redefine your life. As you navigate the unknown, remember that your support system doesn't have to be perfect; it just must be yours. Whether it is a single mentor, a close-knit group of friends, or the resilience you build within yourself, every step forward counts.

Your journey is unique, and so is the network of people and resources that will help you along the way. Trust the process, embrace the lessons, and never underestimate the power of connection. Like a tree rooted in fertile soil, you will grow tall and robust when nourished by the proper support.

In the words of Maya Angelou, "I can be changed by what happens to me. But I refuse to be reduced by it." May this be your mantra as you seek the support system to carry you through your destiny transitions, turning obstacles into stepping stones and challenges into triumphs.

* 10 *

Great Leaders Are Born by the Quality of Their Adversity.

"Adversity shapes leaders, moulds their followers, and transforms their environment. Running from adversity is not just fleeing a challenge; it's forfeiting your destiny."
—S. Olamilekan Isreal,

Adversity is not merely an unwelcome guest. It is the unseen architect of greatness. Running from adversity is not just about avoiding discomfort; it is about turning away from the very process that shapes your destiny.

Adversity and destiny are not enemies; they are partners in the journey. Think of the great leaders who have shaped history. Nelson Mandela's 27 years of imprisonment didn't break his spirit—it strengthened it, refining him for the moment when he would unite a nation. Martin Luther King Jr. faced unrelenting opposition, yet his courage was not just about survival; it was about turning struggle into a purpose that changed the world. These leaders didn't view their trials as obstacles but as stepping stones to something greater.

Adversity is a forge—a place where fear, doubt, and ego are burned away, leaving only the purest form of your potential. Each challenge is like a sculptor's chisel, carving the leader within. The lessons learned through adversity, perseverance, humility, and compassion—become the foundation of a leader's authenticity and depth. Without hardship, leadership is hollow, disconnected from the struggles of those you aim to inspire.

Imagine adversity as a master sculptor. Every trial, setback, and rejection is a deliberate strike of the chisel, carving away fear and ego, revealing the masterpiece within. Without these strikes, you remain incomplete and unshaped. Adversity teaches perseverance in the face of setbacks, humility in moments of failure, and compassion in shared pain. It doesn't just build you. It transforms you into a leader worth following.

Here's the paradox: though adversity is necessary, it is something most of us instinctively avoid. We seek easier paths, running from discomfort. But by avoiding adversity, we are not simply escaping hardship, we are stepping away from our destiny. Each time we flee from a challenge, we deny ourselves the chance to grow into the leader we are meant to become.

Look at any leader who has left a legacy. They have faced storms, rejection, betrayal, and moments of complete despair. But they didn't quit. They embraced the struggle, not because it was easy, but because they understood that adversity was never meant to defeat them, it was there to prepare them.

Adversity is both the source and the seasoning of extraordinary leadership. It gives depth to your journey and substance to your influence. It is the essence of transformation. So, when you find yourself at a crossroads, standing face-to-face with adversity, don't see it as an obstacle. See it as an invitation to step into your destiny. Life is asking, "How far are you willing to go to fulfil your purpose?"

As you lean into discomfort, remember that adversity is not your enemy. It is your ally, shaping you for the greatness that awaits. Without adversity, there is no transition. Without transition, there is no destiny.

The Impact of Destiny Transitions on Legacy

One of the most striking truths about legacy is that it isn't built overnight. It is forged in the crucible of life's transitions, shaped by challenges, perseverance, and the lessons gained. The great leaders we admire today, such as Nelson Mandela, Martin Luther King Jr., and countless others, did not bypass the struggles of their transitional phases. Instead, they embraced them, understanding that these trials were not obstacles but stepping stones towards greatness.

Destiny transitions are not just personal; they are purposeful. They refine us, stretching our potential and giving us the strength to leave a mark on the world. They teach us resilience, self-discipline, and the value of perseverance. And when we embrace these lessons, our lives begin to inspire and impact others, weaving the foundation of a legacy.

Reflecting on my journey, I see how my transitions weren't designed to break me but to build me. They were moments that taught me to rise above fear and self-doubt. The struggles felt overwhelming at times, but in hindsight, they were the building blocks of who I am today. I once wrote, "Self-discipline may feel like pain at first, but the joy of its results is indescribable."

This chapter explores how living with purpose during your transitions creates a ripple effect that impacts generations, how authentic legacies are formed, and why embracing the challenges of destiny transitions is crucial for anyone aspiring to leave an indelible mark on the world.

How Does Living Your Purpose Create a Lasting Impact?

Living your purpose is not just about achieving personal fulfilment; it's about creating a legacy that uplifts and inspires others. One powerful example of this is Bishop David Oyedepo, the founder of the Living Faith Church (Winners' Chapel). Oyedepo's journey was not without struggles. In the early years of his ministry, he faced financial challenges, doubt, and other setbacks. However, his unwavering belief in his God-given purpose kept him moving forward.

Oyedepo's determination during his transitional phases is a testament to how purpose strengthens legacy. His focus on education, empowerment, and spiritual growth has impacted millions globally. Landmark University, Covenant University, and numerous other initiatives under his leadership have transformed lives, proving that living your purpose creates ripples of change far beyond your immediate reach.

Like Oyedepo, your purpose isn't meant to serve you alone. When you embrace your calling and persevere through transitions, you ignite a legacy that inspires others to pursue their paths with courage and faith.

The Ripple Effect of Following Destiny Transitions on Others

Every step you take during your destiny transition has the potential to impact others. Your perseverance becomes a testimony, your growth becomes a guide, and your victories become a vision for those watching.

Consider Rosa Parks, whose quiet act of defiance during the Civil Rights Movement catalysed systemic change. Parks didn't set out to spark a movement; she followed her convictions. But her courage during her transition, standing firm in the face of oppression, ignited a ripple effect that empowered countless others to fight for equality.

You may not always see the immediate impact when you embrace your transitions. However, your determination creates unseen ripples. Your courage inspires others to confront their fears, and your resilience encourages someone else to keep going. Destiny transitions are personal milestones and opportunities to influence, inspire, and uplift those who cross your path.

Examples of Legacies Built on Authentic Purpose

Legacies that stand the test of time are those built on authenticity anchored in a clear, unwavering purpose. These legacies inspire others not because they are perfect but because they are genuine. They reflect the courage to remain steadfast in one's values, even when faced with adversity.

Take the story of Nelson Mandela, whose legacy of reconciliation and justice is rooted in his steadfast commitment to freedom and equality. Mandela's 27 years in prison were not merely years of waiting—they were years of transformation and preparation. Despite unimaginable suffering, he held fast to his purpose, emerging as a global symbol of resilience and forgiveness. His leadership in transitioning South Africa from apartheid to democracy directly resulted from his willingness to endure his destiny transitions gracefully and resolve. Mandela's authenticity and focus on his purpose ensured his legacy would inspire future generations.

Similarly, consider the life of Oprah Winfrey, who transformed personal adversity into a platform of empowerment. Oprah's childhood was marked by poverty and trauma, yet she remained true to her belief in the power of storytelling and connection. She built a media empire and a legacy of inspiration and hope through her authenticity. The authenticity of her purpose—to uplift and empower others—resonates deeply, making her one of the most influential figures of our time.

Another powerful example is Harriet Tubman, who risked her life to lead enslaved people to freedom through the Underground Railroad. Tubman's legacy of courage and selflessness was born from her unwavering purpose: to fight for freedom and justice. Even when the risks were immense, she remained authentic to her calling, ultimately symbolising hope and resilience for generations.

These stories illustrate that legacies built on authentic purpose are not about seeking perfection or avoiding hardship. Instead, they embrace challenges as opportunities to live out one's truth. Authenticity ensures that the impact you leave is deeply rooted in who you are and what you stand for, creating a legacy that inspires others long after you are gone.

Practical Lessons for Building Your Legacy

1. **Stay True to Your Values:** Authentic purpose requires full commitment to your principles. Whether you face setbacks or victories, let your values guide your decisions.
2. **Embrace the Journey:** Challenges during destiny transitions are not roadblocks but stepping stones. The struggles you overcome become the foundation of your legacy.
3. **Inspire Through Action:** Authentic purpose is best demonstrated through consistent action. Your willingness to act on your beliefs will inspire others to do the same.

Destiny transitions are life's way of refining us. They are not meant to break us but to shape us into the individuals we are called to be. Every challenge, moment of self-discipline, and lesson learned is a step towards building a legacy that impacts generations.

Your journey is unique, and so is the mark you will leave. Embrace the process, trust in your purpose, and let the transitions mould you into someone whose life inspires others to rise above their struggles.

Remember, the struggles of today are the testimonies of tomorrow. They are the stories that will inspire others to persevere. They are the bricks with which you build your legacy. As you face your destiny transitions, know that you are not just living for yourself but creating a foundation for those who will come after you. And that is the true impact of destiny transitions on legacy.

Great leaders are born by the quality of their adversity.

Appreciation To You!

Dear Reader,

As you turn the pages of "The Power of Transition," I am filled with excitement and hope for the transformative journey you will embark upon. This book is not just a collection of words; it is a guide, mirror, and companion through life's inevitable transitions.

Transitions are universal yet deeply personal. They come with challenges, triumphs, and growth, reshaping the essence of who we are. Through this book, I aim to illuminate the path, offering insights, strategies, and encouragement to help you navigate these pivotal moments gracefully and purposefully.

This book is from my personal experiences and observations—stories of resilience, setbacks, and breakthroughs. But beyond my journey, it is written with you in mind. Your potential to overcome, grow, and leave a legacy is what drives this work. Every chapter is crafted to inspire, empower, and equip you to face life's transitions head-on, turning obstacles into stepping stones towards greatness.

I urge you to share the lessons and insights from this book with those you care about. When we collectively embrace the power of transitions, we cultivate a culture of understanding, empathy, and progress. Together, we can inspire hope in others who may feel stuck, reminding them that every transition holds the seed of transformation.

Please stay connected with me as we explore these themes beyond the book. Follow us on our social platforms and website, where we share daily inspirations, practical tools, and stories from others who, like you, are navigating life's transitions. Your feedback, experiences, and thoughts mean the world to me—they keep this dialogue alive and meaningful.

Thank you for investing your time in this journey. I believe that "The Power of Transition" will not only inspire but also empower you to embrace change, pursue your dreams, and lead a life filled with purpose and impact.

With gratitude and hope,

S. Olamilekan Isreal

Website: www.olamilekanisreal.com

Acknowledgement

With a heart full of gratitude, I bow to the King of the Universe and the Holy Spirit, whose unfailing wisdom, grace, and strength guided every step of this journey. When my country faced one of its toughest economic challenges, I found the courage to push forward and complete this book—alongside my second book in the same month. This accomplishment is not mine alone; it is a testament to divine guidance that transformed a mere idea into reality.

To my incredible team—Saheed Amoo, Daramola Oluwatosin, Favor Adewuyi, and Mr. Oluwatosin Ajigbotoluwa, thank you for walking this path with me. Your encouragement, belief, and relentless support were the pillars that held me up when the journey felt overwhelming. May the universe reward you with boundless success and fulfilment in all your endeavours.

To my wife, my anchor and source of unwavering support, your belief in me made the impossible seem achievable. Your love and encouragement gave me strength during the darkest moments. This book is as much your victory as it is mine.

To my dear friend and editor, Mr. Kolade Gbolagade, thank you for your steadfast commitment and expert guidance. Your honest feedback and encouragement turned this project into its best version. Your dedication has been invaluable, and I am deeply grateful.

To my friends and family, who have shown me unconditional love and support, your belief in me lifted my spirit on days I questioned my abilities. Though I cannot name everyone here, please know your contributions are etched in my heart and have left a profound mark on this work.

Finally, I take a moment to acknowledge myself. The resilience, determination, and perseverance it took to complete this journey have been a profound lesson in growth and transformation. I am proud of the person I have become through this process.

To everyone who stood by me and contributed to this journey, thank you for helping me realise this dream. This book is a culmination of my efforts and a testament to the power of faith, love, and a resilient spirit.

With endless gratitude,

S. Olamilekan Isreal